Butler Area Public Library

In Memory of
Aunt Madeline Regis Steltzer

Donor
Joanne and Sandy Reges

D1302072

A Special Gift for

_____

with Love

_____

Date

_____

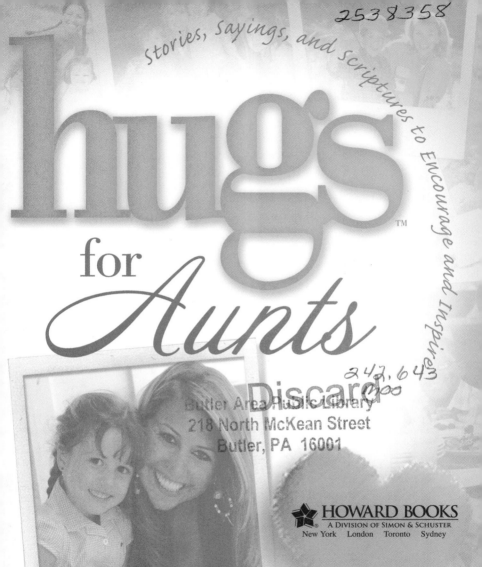

Stories, Sayings, and Scriptures to Encourage and Inspire

hugs™

for Aunts

HOWARD BOOKS
A DIVISION OF SIMON & SCHUSTER
New York   London   Toronto   Sydney

KAREN MOORE
Personalized Scriptures by
LEANN WEISS

Our purpose at Howard Books is to:
• *Increase faith* in the hearts of growing Christians
• *Inspire holiness* in the lives of believers
• *Instill hope* in the hearts of struggling people everywhere
Because He's coming again!

HOWARD
BOOKS

Published by Howard Books, a division of Simon & Schuster, Inc.
1230 Avenue of the Americas, New York, NY 10020
www.howardpublishing.com

Hugs for Aunts © 2007 by Howard Books

Paraphrased scriptures © 2007 by LeAnn Weiss
3006 Brandywine Drive, Orlando, FL 32806
407-898-4410

Library of Congress Cataloging-in-Publication Data
Moore, Karen.
  Hugs for aunts : stories, sayings, and scriptures to encourage and inspire / Karen Moore ; personalized scriptures by LeAnn Weiss.
    p. cm.
  1. Aunts—Religious life. 2. Christian women—Religious life. I. Weiss, LeAnn. II. Title.
  BV4527.M625 2007
  242'.643—dc22

2007021370

ISBN 13: 978-1-4165-4180-6
ISBN 10:   1-4165-4180-2
10 9 8 7 6 5 4 3 2 1

HOWARD and colophon are registered trademarks of Simon & Schuster, Inc.

Manufactured in the United States of America

For information regarding special discounts for bulk purchases, please contact:
Simon & Schuster Special Sales at 1-800-456-6798 or business@simonandschuster.com.

Edited by Between the Lines
Cover design by John Mark Luke Design
Interior design by Tennille Paden
Photography by Chrys Howard

Contents

Chapter One

Aunts Are Wise

You can't begin to fathom My understanding of you. My wisdom is pure, peaceable, considerate, impartial, sincere, and full of mercy. Just ask, and I'll help you to prioritize your days and give you a heart of wisdom.

Teaching you,
Your God of Wisdom
—from Isaiah 40:28; James 3:17; Psalm 90:12

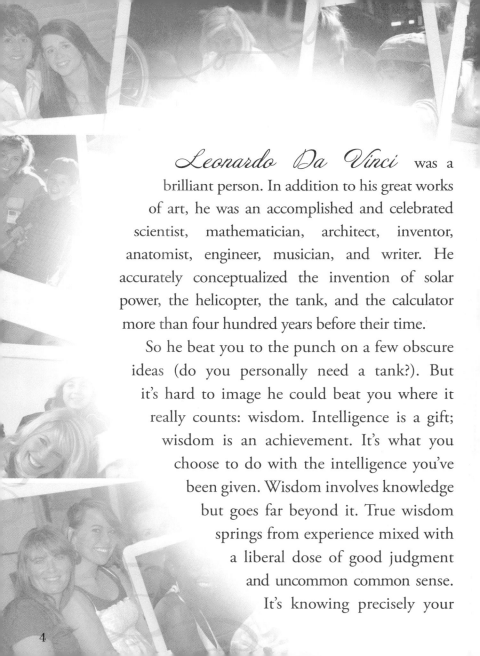

Leonardo Da Vinci was a brilliant person. In addition to his great works of art, he was an accomplished and celebrated scientist, mathematician, architect, inventor, anatomist, engineer, musician, and writer. He accurately conceptualized the invention of solar power, the helicopter, the tank, and the calculator more than four hundred years before their time.

So he beat you to the punch on a few obscure ideas (do you personally need a tank?). But it's hard to image he could beat you where it really counts: wisdom. Intelligence is a gift; wisdom is an achievement. It's what you choose to do with the intelligence you've been given. Wisdom involves knowledge but goes far beyond it. True wisdom springs from experience mixed with a liberal dose of good judgment and uncommon common sense. It's knowing precisely your place, understanding how things fit together, discerning what's appropriate or best, and pursuing excellence.

Some aunts, like you, are inherently wise. They know how the world—and human nature—works. They understand the seductive nature of the temptations before us, the dangers of giving in, and the way to resist. They know what's important in life, what's just gravy, and what's best avoided. They see things about us that even we don't yet know about ourselves, and they gently, kindly, and wisely help us discover it for ourselves and make our own wise choices.

Wisdom isn't something you can teach or bestow: you can only model it, exude it, and hope those around you imbibe and absorb it. With each passing year, we see your wisdom more clearly. Thank you for sharing it with us.

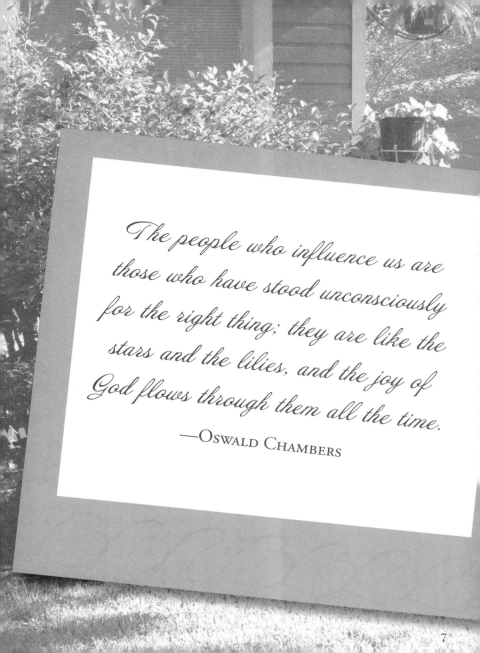

The people who influence us are those who have stood unconsciously for the right thing; they are like the stars and the lilies, and the joy of God flows through them all the time.

—OSWALD CHAMBERS

Everything in Its Place

It almost felt as if she were going home. Katie had always had a fondness for visiting Aunt Margaret's house as a child. She loved the huge yard, the country feel, the colorful plantings, and the big old house with lots of nooks and crannies for exploring. As an only child, she used to climb the big weeping willow tree when she needed a break from her boisterous cousins. Maybe she'd climb up in that tree once again. She certainly could use a break from the boisterous, dizzying life in the big city that was threatening to overwhelm her.

She sighed as she turned down Aunt Margaret's street. She turned off the air conditioning in her Hyundai and rolled down the window, inhaling deeply the sweet country fragrances she remembered from her happy childhood visits. Since each of her parents had remarried in recent months, everything had changed. Katie didn't feel at home—or overly welcome—with either new stepparent. That was why when her heart yearned for home, it was to Aunt Margaret's that she was drawn.

She had barely turned into the gravel drive when the door of the house was flung open and a joyous Aunt Margaret bounced down the steps to greet her, arms open wide. She practically pulled Katie from the car and enveloped her in a safe, comforting hug. Katie dissolved into her aunt's embrace. The faint smell of jasmine, her aunt's trademark scent, made Katie feel both secure and consoled.

"Katie, darling!" Aunt Margaret exclaimed. "It just warms the cockles of my heart to see you again. It's about time you got some of that big-city smog out of your hair."

"I've had about all I can stand for a while." Katie tried to make it sound like a joke, but the laugh she intended stuck in her throat. It was too close to the uncomfortable truth. She'd needed to escape the city, her job—her life. More and more she was worried that she'd made the wrong choices. Maybe Aunt Margaret's decision to live in a small town was wiser than Katie's decision to pursue a fast-paced advertising career in the city. After all, Aunt Margaret had a lovely home and a happy heart, neither of which had come to Katie yet.

Aunt Margaret steered her toward the house. "I can't wait to hear all about your life in the city—your job, your apartment, your friends—everything," she said. "It must be so exciting!"

"My job practically consumes me, my apartment is about the size of your family room, and my friends—well, their lives are pretty exciting, I guess. They all seem to have the right boyfriends, the right apartments—the right lives." Katie forced a chuckle. "Haven't let me in on their secret yet. But let's not talk about that right now. Tell me what's going on with you."

A concerned look crossed Aunt Margaret's face briefly; she studied Katie for a moment, then changed the subject as asked. "Oh, I expect you know how it is," Aunt Margaret said cheerfully. "It's the simple life. Nothing much changes here, but I keep busy . . . happy."

"That's good," Katie replied, setting her suitcase in the entryway and surveying her aunt's home. The house looked like Aunt Margaret: fastidious, neat, totally pulled together. Everything in the house looked like it was made to be exactly where it was, not one item out of place. Katie pulled a windblown piece of hair out of her eyes and wedged it behind her ear. Aunt Margaret had been out in the wind too, but not a single hair was out of place. How did she manage? Katie wondered.

"I've got some people coming over for a barbecue," Aunt Margaret announced.

Inwardly, Katie groaned. She'd come to relax and get away from stress. The last thing she wanted was to make small talk with a bunch of strangers. "Oh, I didn't mean to come at a bad time," Katie apologized. "I'll go for a drive or stay in my room to keep out of your way."

"Nonsense," Aunt Margaret said firmly. "I've told everyone you're coming. Some haven't seen you since you were knee-high to a grasshopper. Others are anxious to meet you after hearing me brag about you. Besides," she added with a twinkle in her eye, "I'll need your help to pull it together."

It would never do for Aunt Margaret to host a party that wasn't as pulled together as she was. Seemed Katie was in, whether she liked it or not.

"There you are." Aunt Margaret sat down on the porch swing beside Katie. "Did you try my homemade strawberry-rhubarb pie?" she asked, pushing the pie plate toward Katie, who fended it off.

"Oh yes," Katie said, rubbing her stomach, "and the pecan and the lemon meringue. I'm so full I could burst! And the barbecue chicken . . . corn on the cob . . . everything was delicious. Aunt Margaret, you are an outstanding cook."

Aunt Margaret laughed appreciatively. "I'm glad you enjoyed it." She was silent for a moment, then asked cautiously, "Have you enjoyed anything else about the day?"

"Oh yes!" Katie hugged her knees to her chest happily. "It's been a delightful day. Everybody's been friendly and kind. They all like and respect you, Aunt Margaret. It seems like such a welcoming, close-knit community. I almost forget myself and feel at home."

Encouraged by Aunt Margaret's understanding smile and a slight squeeze on her elbow, Katie continued. "Remember that neighbor boy, Josh, who chased me with frogs when I was six? He's all grown up—and pretty nicely."

Her aunt chuckled.

"Did you know his father, Randolph, is the mayor?" Katie enthused.

"I know." Aunt Margaret's eyes seemed to dance.

"He seems pretty nice too."

"Yes, he certainly does."

"Josh is a photographer who teaches at the local college," Katie continued. "He really seems to love what he does."

"That's important," Aunt Margaret said.

Katie was silent for a long moment. "He told me there's an opening at the college for an advertising instructor," she confided softly. "He encouraged me to apply for it."

"Why Katie, that's wonderful!" Aunt Margaret exulted. "Are you interested?"

Katie sighed wearily. "It's mighty tempting," she conceded. "I've always loved being here with you, Aunt Margaret. You make me feel at home. And after spending the afternoon with your wonderful neighbors, I can almost imagine how happy I would feel to truly belong somewhere like this. But . . . "

"But what?" Aunt Margaret pressed gently.

"How do I know where I really belong? I always thought a career in advertising was what I wanted, but now . . . now I'm not so sure . . . about anything. I just feel so locked in to things—too committed for good or bad to make such a big change."

"Do you like where you are now? What you're doing, who you are?"

"Not really," Katie miserably admitted at her aunt's prodding. "But maybe it's my own fault. Maybe I haven't given it enough of a chance. Maybe I'm doing something wrong." She pulled a long lock of hair away from her eyes and stuck it behind her ear, leaned forward earnestly, and continued, "Aunt Margaret, do you think it's possible for your dreams to change? Do you think you can try something for a while and realize it's not the right place or the right job anymore—and make a change?"

"Come here," Aunt Margaret commanded, setting the pie on the porch railing, slipping her arm through Katie's, and steering her to the far end of the porch. From this vantage point Katie could see the whole beautiful yard, including about a dozen guests still milling around the dessert table, chatting, or playing badminton. She saw Josh standing beside his father, talking. He noticed her looking in their direction, smiled, and waved. Katie waved back and hoped he was too far away to see that she was blushing.

"Over there, by the garage. See my beautiful azaleas blooming?"

"They're lovely," Katie agreed. "Several of your neighbors and I were remarking on them earlier."

"I used to have all my azaleas out front," Aunt Margaret continued. "Do you remember coming for Easter and seeing them all abloom?"

"I remember," Katie answered. "They looked like they belonged perfectly out there. Why did you move them?"

"Things changed. A big ice storm a couple winters ago brought down the big spruce out there. With it gone, the azaleas struggled.

They don't do well in direct sun," Aunt Margaret explained. "But once Randolph helped me move them—yes, dear, he's quite a gardener—to a more suitable shady spot out back, they took off, and now they seem quite happy."

Katie leaned across the porch railing and studied the brightly colored azaleas thoughtfully. "I understand what you're saying," she said. "And it gives me hope—and a tiny bit of courage—that I might be able to make a change for the better. But how can I know if my new choice will be any better than my last one?"

"A wise and experienced gardener has a pretty good idea where a particular plant might thrive." Aunt Margaret put her hand on Katie's back reassuringly. "I've sensed for a long time that you know you don't belong in the city. You're like a fish out of water. You belong in a place where your heart feels at home and where you know you're loved. You deserve to be happy, Katie. What does your heart tell you?"

"My heart is telling me that I'd like to at least explore the opportunity at the college Josh mentioned."

"Marvelous! I thought you might discover something to your liking here today."

"You did, did you?" Katie pretended to be offended. "Did you set this whole thing up on my account? You did, didn't you!"

Aunt Margaret winked. "I've been around long enough to know how to arrange a few flowers that seem to go together."

As they walked arm in arm back to their guests, a question suddenly came to Katie. "Aunt Margaret, don't azaleas bloom in early spring? How do you get these to bloom in the middle of summer?"

"They're Encore Azaleas," Aunt Margaret explained. "Just when you think they're through flowering, they get a second wind and bloom all over again."

"Admiring the beautiful azaleas?" Randolph asked as they passed by the mayor and his handsome son.

"Oh yes," Katie agreed. "Aunt Margaret put in a good word for you, bragging about your gardening skills."

"Well, I hope you'll put in a good word for me with your Aunt Margaret," he said with a wink.

Katie was surprised to see Aunt Margaret blush and instantly suspected—no, knew—what Randolph meant. She smiled and raised one eyebrow as if to say, "You and the mayor?"

Aunt Margaret sweetly whispered, "Azaleas aren't the only ones that can have an encore."

Katie slipped her arm out of Aunt Margaret's and into Josh's. "I suddenly have a strong desire to take a look at that college of yours," she said with a self-assurance that astounded and delighted her. "Would you be willing to take me on a tour of the campus?"

"I'd be delighted," he said with a smile that seemed strong and genuine. She looked back and locked eyes with Aunt Margaret, who was smiling broadly. As Katie turned back, a gust of wind blew her hair. Instinctively, she reached up to push the stray hair from her face but then realized there was no need. For once, everything seemed to be right where it belonged.

Chapter Two

Aunts Give

Remember, I'm the Source of every good and perfect gift. Cheerful giving brings joy to My heart. When you give, I will fill your life to overflowing with blessings. You can trust Me to provide for all of your needs. Take advantage of My compassion and tender mercies, which are waiting for you each morning.

Giving you abundant life,
Your Heavenly Father
—from James 1:17; 2 Corinthians 9:7; Luke 6:38; Philippians 4:19; Lamentations 3:22–23

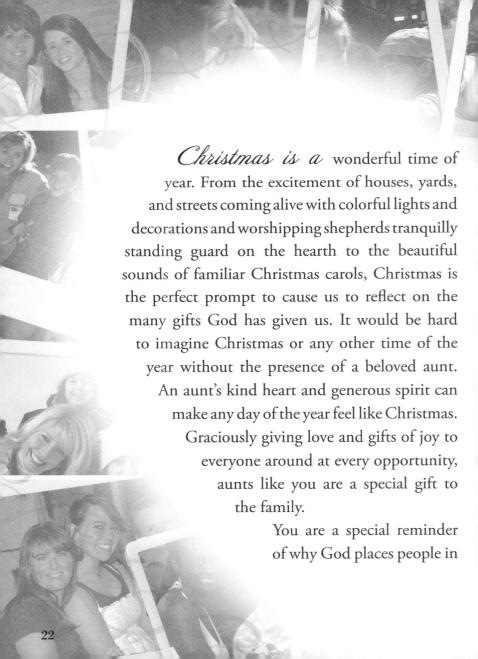

Christmas is a wonderful time of year. From the excitement of houses, yards, and streets coming alive with colorful lights and decorations and worshipping shepherds tranquilly standing guard on the hearth to the beautiful sounds of familiar Christmas carols, Christmas is the perfect prompt to cause us to reflect on the many gifts God has given us. It would be hard to imagine Christmas or any other time of the year without the presence of a beloved aunt. An aunt's kind heart and generous spirit can make any day of the year feel like Christmas. Graciously giving love and gifts of joy to everyone around at every opportunity, aunts like you are a special gift to the family.

You are a special reminder of why God places people in

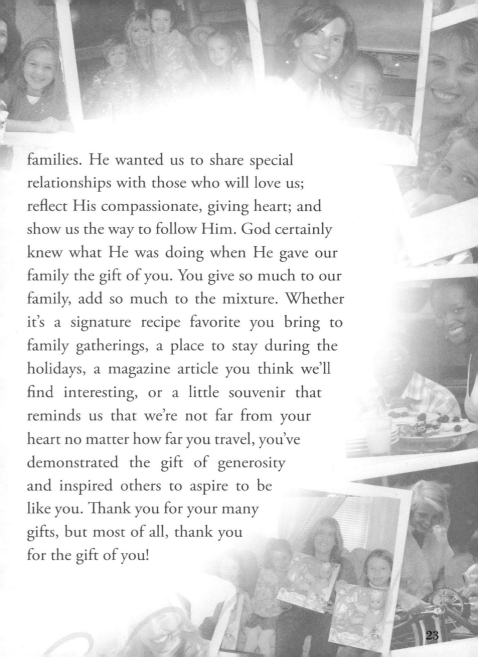

families. He wanted us to share special relationships with those who will love us; reflect His compassionate, giving heart; and show us the way to follow Him. God certainly knew what He was doing when He gave our family the gift of you. You give so much to our family, add so much to the mixture. Whether it's a signature recipe favorite you bring to family gatherings, a place to stay during the holidays, a magazine article you think we'll find interesting, or a little souvenir that reminds us that we're not far from your heart no matter how far you travel, you've demonstrated the gift of generosity and inspired others to aspire to be like you. Thank you for your many gifts, but most of all, thank you for the gift of you!

The manner of giving shows the character of the giver, more than the gift itself.

—Johann Kaspar Lavater

Auntie Claus

"Why won't Santa come here this year?" Margie's wide eyes reflected the shock and disbelief her younger sister, Elena, had felt when their mother made the sad pronouncement. "Doesn't he know where we live?" Margie pressed. "Maybe we're too far out in the country. Should I send him a letter?"

Margie was eight and knew a lot more about these things than Elena did. At only four, Elena could write just her name and a few special words, but writing a letter sounded like a hopeful idea. Other people had trouble finding the house: it was certainly possible that Santa might not be able to find them on their country road on top of the hill. Margie could write well, and a letter giving Santa directions just might be the thing to do.

"I was going to make Santa a card," ventured six-year-old Ruthie, her eyes welling with tears.

Their mom looked at her three little girls and sighed. "I'm sorry, girls, but it's been a hard winter already, and your daddy is doing his best to take care of us. We just won't be able to invite Santa this year. We'll have fun, though, and we'll make cookies. Okay? Maybe you could each think of one way to help decorate our tree. Daddy will be bringing it in soon."

The girls shook their heads, trying to take in the bad news. Something just wasn't right. Elena knew there was more to Christmas than Santa and presents. In Sunday school she'd learned all about its being the birthday of Jesus, and her class was making up a special song to sing at the Christmas service. Still, she so wanted Santa to come to their house. If she sang really well, maybe God would tell Santa to stop at her house anyway. She comforted herself with the thought.

Elena's house had been built about one hundred and fifty years ago. It had lots of rooms, many of which were closed off to help conserve the heat. Her mom cooked at a big, old, metal stove. During summer she grew vegetables in an enormous garden, then canned and preserved them so they could be eaten throughout the winter. She even made maple syrup from the trees in the spring. To a four-year-old, it seemed like the perfect place to live—except when the winds blew the doors open and made them all have to scramble for warm quilts, or when the snow piled up too high to get out of the driveway. The girls' father worked at a factory, but for some reason he had been home a lot lately. Elena didn't know why.

Elena, Margie, and Ruthie made all kinds of ornaments for the tree. Their mom gave them some Popsicle sticks and juice-can lids to decorate. They had some sparkling glitter and glue and even some pictures from magazines to help create their own designs. Elena made a cute Popsicle-stick donkey that she imagined carrying Baby Jesus to Bethlehem. Her mom gave her a little square of real cloth to put over the stick so it looked like a baby blanket. Everyone said it was a very special ornament. Elena was pleased.

When it was finally time for the Christmas Eve service, Elena was excited. She had worked hard on her song, and her sisters had worked hard on their parts too. Their mom had helped make costumes for each of them. The tiny Methodist church was warm and cozy. Margie portrayed the Virgin Mary in the nativity play, and Ruthie was a shepherd girl. It all went smoothly, and none of them forgot the verses they had to recite. Nice ladies from the church gave out little presents to all the kids, and they served hot chocolate and doughnuts too. All in all, Elena had a fun time.

When the five-o'clock service ended, Elena crunched through the snow with her sisters and father, walking back up the hill to their house. It had started snowing again, so the walk was a little difficult. She clutched the small book of children's prayers she'd been given at Sunday school, along with her candy cane, but her focus was on something far more serious and important. In the program she had sung her heart out for God and hoped He knew why. She held Margie's hand as they trudged along, singing snippets of Christmas carols.

Mom greeted the girls at the door. "I just got home from work," she said, helping them off with their coats. "I'm so sorry I had to miss your program. How did it go?"

"I sang so God could hear me," Elena said solemnly. "I asked Him to send Santa to our house—even if he just dropped off a little tiny present. Was that okay, Mom?"

Elena's mom gave her a hug and helped her get her boots off. "I'm sure it's fine," she said. "Get ready for dinner. Aunt Betty and Uncle Dan should be coming soon."

Elena loved Aunt Betty. She was tall and pretty and always smiled warmly. She talked a little funny. Her mom had told her that was because she lived in the south for so long.

Elena listened anxiously for Aunt Betty and Uncle Dan's car for a long time. After a while, she started to worry that they weren't coming after all. Maybe the snow was falling too fast and would discourage them from visiting. Elena hoped not. She wanted to tell Aunt Betty that Santa wouldn't be coming. Maybe Aunt Betty would have an idea of how to get in touch with him.

Just then she heard a knock at the door and heard her mother rushing to open it. Elena and her sisters ran toward the door in excitement. There stood Aunt Betty and Uncle Dan. "We couldn't get our car up the hill, so we walked a bit," she said, smiling. "I've never seen such snow down south, y'all." She shivered. "I'm glad I brought this fleecy coat."

Elena ran to hug Aunt Betty. "Aunt Betty!" she cried. "Did you know that Santa can't come to see us this year? We're not sure if he can find us up here on this dirt road. Margie wrote a letter to him, but I don't know if he got it."

Aunt Betty knelt down to meet the four-year-old at eye level and hugged Elena. "Well, sweetie," she said, "I'm so sorry to hear that news. I don't think you should worry, though, because I have a pretty good idea about what happened."

"You do?" Elena asked breathlessly. She and her sisters stood watching Aunt Betty and wondering what she could possibly know. They hadn't noticed Uncle Dan discreetly slipping back outside.

Before Aunt Betty could continue, she was interrupted by Uncle

Dan's arrival. This time he was carrying a big box. Aunt Betty's eyes gleamed. "You know," she said, "the funniest thing happened. Santa Claus left this box at my house."

Elena's eyes grew big as saucers.

"Santa told Uncle Dan that he wasn't quite sure how to reach you this year," Aunt Betty continued. "You know Santa likes to be sure all the gifts are delivered. He wouldn't want you to miss Christmas! So he asked if we'd be able to deliver his presents to you girls. I guess he couldn't get up the hill either."

Elena clapped her hands and jumped up and down. Her song had made a difference, she was sure of it. God *did* care that Santa visited her family.

Margie and Ruthie squealed in delight and danced around excitedly. Uncle Dan grinned from ear to ear. Aunt Betty hugged all the girls. Elena's mom had tears in her eyes. Their dad suggested that the girls take the box of gifts and put them under the tree, which wore draping strings of popcorn garland. The girls ran off to do so in delight. As they found gifts with their names on them, they called out to one another: "Here's one for me!" "Hey, here's one for you!"

Because of the snow, Aunt Betty and Uncle Dan ended up staying overnight, so they were all together on Christmas morning. Elena's mother gave each of the girls a glass of juice and brought out coffee for the adults. Then they all gathered around the tree and said a prayer of thanks for the many blessings God had given them. Elena and her sisters each received baby dolls, complete with bottles and pink bonnets; little purses with matching gloves to wear to church; and warm Christmas pajamas. Elena's were pink with satiny ribbons, Ruthie's were green plaid with red reindeer faces, and Margie's were blue with scarf-sporting snowmen. The girls were excited and ran around the room giving hugs to whoever was closest to them.

A few extra surprises still awaited them. They were thrilled to find a new dress that their mom had made. She was a good seamstress, and she knew how to embroider teddy bears and flowers on just the right spots to make each dress special. Ruthie had made Christmas cards for her mom and dad and each of her sisters. She'd even made a special one for Aunt Betty and Uncle Dan just the night before. Their dad gave them each little stockings stuffed with oranges and maple sugar candy.

Aunt Betty and Uncle Dan had brought gifts for the girls' parents as well. Elena's mom laughed when she saw her own new flannel pajamas and a fabulous new cookbook. New winter gloves and a matching scarf brought a bright smile to her dad's face. As they finished opening presents, Elena took her special ornament off the tree. She handed it to Aunt Betty. "Aunt Betty," she said shyly, "I think this ornament is for you. It's a donkey that brought Baby Jesus and His mother to Bethlehem. Without Him, there wouldn't have been a Christmas." She paused thoughtfully, then added softly, "Just like you this year."

Aunt Betty took the cherished ornament from Elena's hands. Elena could see the love in her eyes as she looked at it. "Is this really for me?" she asked. "It's the most beautiful ornament I've ever seen. It will go on my tree as soon as I get home." Aunt Betty gave Elena a warm hug.

In spite of her fears, it actually had turned out to be the best Christmas ever, Elena decided. It brought an answer to prayer, and it brought "Auntie Claus."

Chapter Three

Aunts Make a Difference

Never forget that I am for you! I'm your Way,
your Truth, and your Life. When you trust in
Me wholeheartedly and acknowledge Me in all
that you do, I'll direct your life. With Me on your
side, the seemingly impossible becomes possible.
Even when you don't realize it, I'm working
behind the scenes for you. Watch Me do far
beyond all that you can ask or dream.

Making a way for you,
Your Awesome God

—from Romans 8:31; John 14:6; Proverbs 3:5–6;
Mark 10:27; Ephesians 3:20

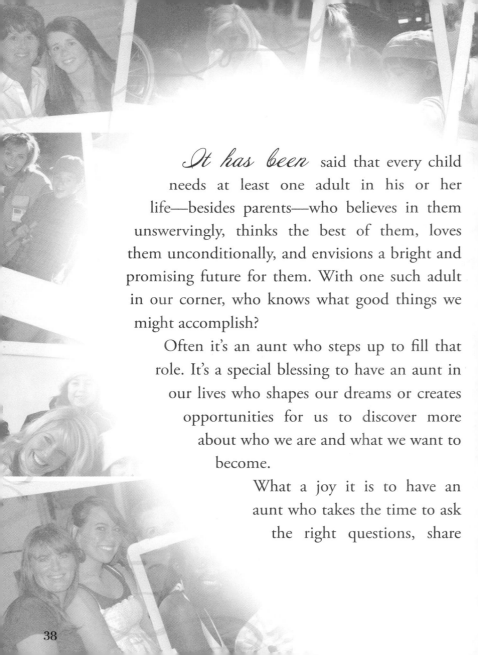

It has been said that every child needs at least one adult in his or her life—besides parents—who believes in them unswervingly, thinks the best of them, loves them unconditionally, and envisions a bright and promising future for them. With one such adult in our corner, who knows what good things we might accomplish?

Often it's an aunt who steps up to fill that role. It's a special blessing to have an aunt in our lives who shapes our dreams or creates opportunities for us to discover more about who we are and what we want to become.

What a joy it is to have an aunt who takes the time to ask the right questions, share

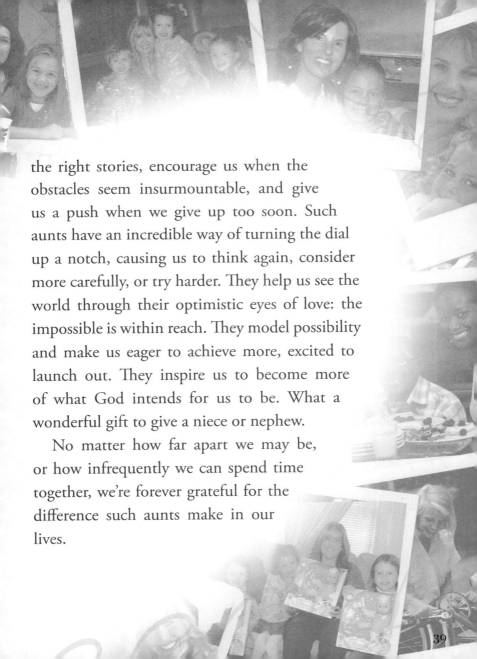

the right stories, encourage us when the obstacles seem insurmountable, and give us a push when we give up too soon. Such aunts have an incredible way of turning the dial up a notch, causing us to think again, consider more carefully, or try harder. They help us see the world through their optimistic eyes of love: the impossible is within reach. They model possibility and make us eager to achieve more, excited to launch out. They inspire us to become more of what God intends for us to be. What a wonderful gift to give a niece or nephew.

No matter how far apart we may be, or how infrequently we can spend time together, we're forever grateful for the difference such aunts make in our lives.

Even if it's a little thing, do something for those who have need of help, something for which you get not pay but the privilege of doing it.

—ALBERT SCHWEITZER

A Tree Full of Doughnuts

Natalie shuffled her feet and realized she didn't know just what to say to the woman standing at the door holding suitcases. Her mother's sister had always been larger than life. *"My sister has a PhD and is a brilliant woman,"* her mother's voice echoed in her mind. *"Now, Natalie, if you just work hard, you could end up like your aunt Meredith."*

Natalie had always thought she'd like to be a bit like Aunt Meredith, but she didn't see how she'd ever measure up. Aunt Meredith was smart and educated: she taught at a university in Idaho and traveled the world, learning, teaching, and speaking. How could Natalie ever hope to compete with that? She wasn't even going to be able to go to college. It would take a lot of money to get the education necessary to lead a life like Aunt Meredith's.

Money and time, apparently. Aunt Meredith had kept busy. Though Natalie had gotten birthday cards from her aunt over the years, she didn't feel like she really knew her. She suddenly worried whether her aunt would even like her. Compared to this adventuresome, accomplished woman, Natalie wasn't anything special.

"Natalie!" Her mother's voice brought her back to the present. "Aren't you going to say hello to your Aunt Meredith and let her in the door?"

Natalie forced a smile and was just stepping forward to give her aunt a little hug when she suddenly found herself enveloped in the biggest, warmest embrace she'd ever experienced in her fifteen years.

"Why, Natalie, dear," Aunt Meredith gushed, "what a fabulous young woman you've become. She has your smile, Sylvia."

Natalie returned her aunt's hug. As her dad and mother stepped out of the room to put Meredith's suitcases in the guest room, she shyly held out a gift, wrapped in patterned tissue paper, to her aunt. "I've made something for you," she said with a smile. "It's one of my favorite memories of you."

Actually, Natalie had to admit, it was just about the only real memory she had of her strong-willed aunt. She hadn't seen her since she was five years old, though it was sometimes difficult for Natalie to separate the real memories from the larger-than-life stories told about Aunt Meredith by other members of the family. Even that vivid memory of the doughnut tree—the image she'd drawn for Aunt Meredith—seemed surreal, an indecipherable combination of actual events and the unreliable haze of sweet childhood memories. A doughnut tree—how could that be? And yet it was. She had seen it . . . lived it . . . it would be forever etched in her mind and linked with Aunt Meredith. Natalie could still conjure the feel of the breeze, the nutmeg-and-sugar aroma of the doughnuts, and the fairy-tale way they looked swaying on the branches of the big tree outside Grandma's farmhouse as they dried in the breeze.

Grandma made the "spudnuts," doughnuts made with potato flour, from an old family recipe each year. Aunt Meredith was the fry cook, and Natalie's mother, Sylvia, was the glazer. To help the doughnuts dry faster, they would hang them, briefly, on the branches of the old tree out front. As the breeze did its work, glaze dripped off those spudnuts onto the ground—or onto whomever was standing below. Natalie and all her cousins were sternly warned to leave the doughnuts alone until they were invited to have one.

The incredible, irresistible smell of those doughnuts nearly made a kid crazy. Natalie remembered that just as one of her cousins started scheming up ways to climb the tree and snatch a doughnut, Aunt Meredith had charged out the door with a stick in her hand, yelling at the top of her lungs. And they were powerful lungs. The stick was supposed to be used as a drying rod for another row of hot pastries, but Aunt Meredith wasn't above using it on a kid's behind first.

All the children scattered at Meredith's approach, except Natalie. Her eyes were as wide open as the doughnut holes. Some frosting had dripped on her finger, and she held it up to Aunt Meredith. She could see her aunt trying to shift gears from the angry woman who'd stormed out of the house after a bunch of unruly boys to a softer one now looking at an awestruck little girl with a glazed finger. Aunt Meredith drew her sizable frame close to Natalie and gave her a squeeze. "You mind Grandma's doughnuts out here, sugar, and I'll see that you get one real soon. We have to make sure we have enough for the church craft festival. Okay?"

Aunt Meredith turned and raised her stick out in warning toward the crouching boys and then headed back to the kitchen and the deep fryer.

When Natalie finally got a fresh, air-dried doughnut, the taste was indescribably wonderful; but it would always be eclipsed in her mind by the powerful image of Aunt Meredith resolutely guarding the sweet treasures of that tree full of doughnuts.

"It's Mom's old farmhouse—and that old tree full of doughnuts!" Aunt Meredith exclaimed when she saw the picture. "Natalie, did you do this? It's wonderful. These doughnuts look as fresh and enticing as the day they were made—like I could just pick one off the tree right now. What a wonderful memory, and a marvelous gift!"

Embarrassed but pleased, Natalie ducked her head. "I'm glad you like it."

"Oh, I do," Aunt Meredith assured her. "But I was talking about you. You're obviously a gifted artist."

"Natalie has been drawing ever since she could hold a crayon," her mother added proudly. "She's won several awards at school for her artwork." Natalie blushed but was thrilled with the high praise from her mother and her much-admired aunt.

At suppertime that night, Natalie listened in awe to her aunt's stories of visiting Germany and Spain and teaching botany and physics. Except for a passing acquaintance with these things in high school classes, Natalie didn't know much about the topics.

"You know so much," Natalie said admiringly. "I wish I knew even half of what you know."

"You'll learn," Aunt Meredith said confidently. "In college . . . where do you plan to go?"

The question just assumed that Natalie would continue her education. Natalie didn't know how to answer without disappointing or offending her aunt. Visions of the bellowing woman from long ago, carrying a big stick and tearing out the front door and off the porch, kept Natalie from responding.

She looked at her aunt and then to her mother. Aunt Meredith looked around the table, and for a moment everyone seemed frozen. Her father put down his fork without eating another bite of mashed potatoes. Her mother attempted a smile. Then her father asked for more mashed potatoes and mumbled something about gravy.

"Natalie probably won't go to college, Meredith," her mother finally explained. "We just don't think there's any way we'll be able to afford it. Natalie understands that, don't you, dear?"

It was obvious that Aunt Meredith didn't understand. She pushed her chair back, stood up, and walked over to stand beside Natalie. "Now tell me, Natalie. What would you like to be when you grow up? What do you think God made you to be?"

Natalie looked around the table at her family and then back at her aunt. "Well, I guess I love more than anything to draw and paint."

"Yes," Meredith murmured approvingly. "The picture of the doughnut tree was outstanding."

"Would you like to see other pieces I've been working on?" Natalie ventured.

Aunt Meredith beamed. "Absolutely."

When Natalie returned to the table, she had a bulging portfolio of her artwork in charcoals and pastels. As Aunt Meredith leafed through the pages, she studied the pieces carefully. "Good use of color . . . nice details and perspective . . . unusual technique here . . . such emotion and movement you've captured. Yes, yes, yes!"

With tears in her eyes, Aunt Meredith responded directly to Natalie. "Child, I truly believe this is your calling. I'm convinced you are meant to praise God with your artwork." Then she turned to her sister and brother-in-law. "This is Natalie's gift to the world. Whatever we have to do, this girl has got to go to college so she can develop her gift with the best training."

Hope rose in Natalie's heart, but she kept it in check, not wanting to be disappointed . . . not wanting to hurt or burden her parents, who had said they couldn't afford college. "But college costs too much," she protested.

"Costs too much *not* to go," Aunt Meredith responded. "Lots of scholarships are out there for girls with talent and good grades." She looked pointedly at Natalie, who got the message. She'd study harder than ever. "And then there are internship programs for high schoolers . . . grants, advanced placement, loans. I've got lots of connections. I'll start working on it as soon as I get home. I'm almost certain we can find something to cover at least half the tuition." She glanced around the table once again. "What do you think you could do about the rest of that amount?"

Natalie spoke first: "I'll work really hard to qualify for a scholarship." She was uncertain how her parents might respond to Aunt Meredith's pressing. But they seemed to have caught her enthusiasm as well. Her mom said she'd been saving her earnings from the beautiful crocheted pieces she sold every year at local craft stores. She had planned to surprise Natalie with this gift at her high-school graduation, but she was pleased to let her know about it now. Natalie immediately got up from the table and hugged her mom with joy.

Her dad said he knew someone at work who might be willing to give Natalie a summer job helping in his wife's gift shop. Maybe Natalie could even display her artwork. He had actually talked about Natalie's artwork to the store's owner in the past.

Natalie let out a happy shriek and clapped her hands, then hugged Aunt Meredith as hard as she could. She was starting to believe it was truly possible. She had never imagined such a conversation would take place in her house. She'd been too afraid to ask her family for solutions about going to college because she didn't want to burden them with her hopes and dreams. She gave her aunt a warm smile as they continued to talk, plot, and dream long into the night.

Natalie sent up some prayers of thanksgiving to God for her aunt and this amazing turn of events. How nice to think that a tree full of doughnuts was helping to shape her life's story. She felt her eyes glazing over with warm tears.

Chapter Four

Aunts Are Heroes

I am your sun and your shield. I give you kindness and honor. I lavish your life with good things when you practice virtue. The path of the righteous is like the first gleam of dawn. May your life shine brighter each day.

Watching over you,
Your All-Powerful God
—from Psalm 84:11; Proverbs 4:18

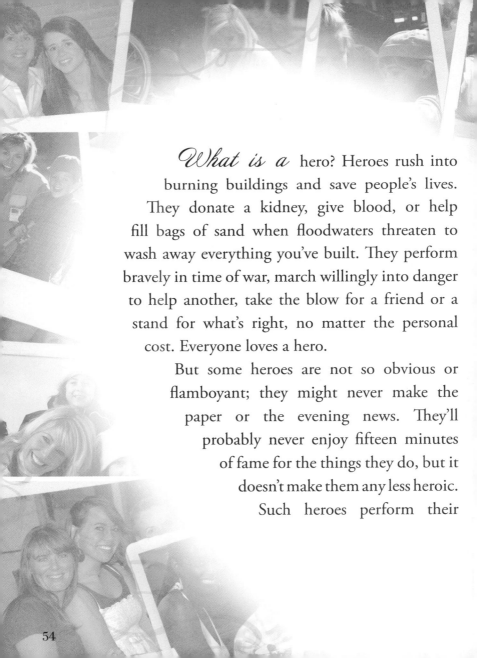

What is a hero? Heroes rush into burning buildings and save people's lives. They donate a kidney, give blood, or help fill bags of sand when floodwaters threaten to wash away everything you've built. They perform bravely in time of war, march willingly into danger to help another, take the blow for a friend or a stand for what's right, no matter the personal cost. Everyone loves a hero.

But some heroes are not so obvious or flamboyant; they might never make the paper or the evening news. They'll probably never enjoy fifteen minutes of fame for the things they do, but it doesn't make them any less heroic. Such heroes perform their valiant deeds on a daily basis: they save us from burning doubts that damage our self-esteem; they free us from self-recrimination; they bravely stand with us when the world turns against us; they give us hope when circumstances seem hopeless.

Did you know that "hero" is often in an aunt's job description? Hero aunts earn their "wings" in many different ways, but it all boils down to the same basic concept: aunts who love us, are there for us, stand behind us, go before us, show us a good example, inspire us, and strengthen us when we're weak—these are the aunts who are truly heroes. You deserve a medal, dear aunt. For truly you are one of the great heroes to those who love you.

I feel the capacity to care gives life its deepest significance.

—PABLO CASALS

Great-Aunt Sarah

Never before had Sarah been so relieved for a ride to end. The pain in her left hip made intolerable by the jarring bumps of her neglected driveway subsided into a dull ache as she waited for her grandnephew, Frank, to retrieve her wheelchair from the trunk of the car. She studied the house and yard intently. It looked basically as she'd left it—the grass was greener and a bit too long, and the pussy willows and forsythias were past their prime. She'd missed having seen them at their glorious peak. Still, somehow everything seemed different, empty, foreign to her. She could still remember what it felt like to belong here, but she knew she would never really feel that way again.

The Rainbow Senior Center was her home now. She hated that thought just as she hated the place. Not that it was a bad place, as far as homes like that went, Sarah admitted. It just wasn't what she'd been planning. She had planned to enlarge her strawberry bed this year, grow award-winning watermelons, and can fifty-two quarts of tomatoes—one for each Sunday's batch of spaghetti. Even in her nineties, Sarah was feisty—in good health, independent, with lots to do and see. But that was before she'd broken her hip; everything had changed in an instant.

"How are we going to get her up the steps?" Sarah overheard Frank's new wife, MaryAnn, asking him.

"I can handle it." Frank sounded annoyed by the question.

That had been the problem for Sarah, though. She would never again be able to handle living here by herself. Too many stairs: the front porch, the basement, and the second floor. Even if her hip eventually healed perfectly, such obstacles were increasingly likely to cause another fall. *Oh well*, she consoled herself sardonically. *I've heard that many old women only live a few months after breaking a hip.* She sighed wearily. *I guess I can put up with almost anything for that long.*

But she wasn't relishing this day—closing up the house and going through her things, deciding what she could keep, what should be given to various relatives, and what would be sold along with her house at an estate sale. She was grateful to Frank and MaryAnn for their help, but she knew it would be a long and emotional day. She steeled herself against the pain—physical and emotional—as Frank opened the car door and prepared to lift her into the wheelchair.

Sarah sat in her favorite overstuffed chair—she'd almost forgotten how good it felt—and pronounced judgment on the items Frank and MaryAnn brought before her. It had been difficult at first, but she'd grown increasingly efficient and ruthless in disposing of her possessions and memories as the afternoon wore on. Rather than wearing her down, clearing things out gave Sarah an unexpected feeling of empowerment and control. In fact, it surprised her to realize that getting rid of the old things seemed harder on Frank than it was on her. He said it was because he'd spent so many afternoons here after school, waiting for his mother to pick him up on her way home from work, but Sarah suspected he was mostly just feeling bad for her. Such a kind, sensitive boy he'd always been, Sarah recalled with pride. She wished her sister had lived to see her only grandson grow to honorable manhood. She would have loved him as dearly as Sarah did herself.

"Have a look at this, Aunt Sarah," Frank interrupted her thoughts as he lugged a large camel-topped chest to a spot beside her chair.

MaryAnn moved closer with obvious interest. Sarah gently rubbed her fingers across the dusty surface of the lid, uncovering the ancient engraving: S.A.D. 1944.

"Who's S.A.D.?" MaryAnn asked eagerly.

"I am." Sarah's response was almost inaudible. "At least, I was."

"Sarah Arlene Davidson," Frank explained. "It's the trunk Aunt Sarah had when she was an army nurse in World War II. She didn't marry Uncle Matthew and become a Langhorne until sometime after the war."

Frank carefully opened the lid, revealing Sarah's army nursing cap and uniform. She picked it up and examined it fondly. s. a. davidson was stamped on the pocket, and a small gold cross was still pinned to the lapel. She set the cap atop her head while holding the uniform up under her chin. "How do I look?" she asked mischievously.

"Wonderful." Frank leaned down and planted a kiss on her wrinkled cheek.

"Wow." MaryAnn sounded genuinely impressed. "I never knew you were a hero."

"I told you she was a hero," Frank sounded defensive.

"Well, yeah," MaryAnn admitted. "But I thought you meant because she took care of you, loved you, and helped you through school. But a real war hero . . . "

"Not a hero." Sarah laughed. "Just an army nurse."

"Don't be modest," Frank chided. "Aunt Sarah was a flight nurse. She took special training to be prepared to care for wounded soldiers on flights where there was high risk for crash landings."

"Planes in those days weren't especially reliable," Aunt Sarah explained. "Just turning on the heater could cause the engine to blow. Pilots had to make tough decisions: turn it on and put all their lives in danger or leave it off and risk freezing the wounded men."

"Not many nurses opted to take on the extra hardships and risk that came with such an assignment," Frank added proudly.

"Did you ever have any close calls?" MaryAnn asked, her eyes narrowed with interest.

"Well . . . " Sarah stroked her chin thoughtfully. "Once I was on a transport plane en route to Guadalcanal with twenty-four litter patients; you know, patients who had to be restrained for some reason. We ran out of fuel over the Pacific, and the pilot had to find a place to land in that vast ocean. He spotted a small island with clearing of about a hundred and fifty feet around some coconut palm trees. He decided it was a better shot than putting it down in the ocean, so he made for it."

MaryAnn gasped supportively while Sarah continued. "'Hold on tight,' the pilot told us. Well, we had a rough landing, but everyone survived. One wounded soldier had his windpipe severed in the landing. Fortunately, his jugular vein was intact, and I was able to improvise a syringe from a tube on a life jacket to keep the blood out of his windpipe until help arrived."

"Oh, my," MaryAnn sympathized. "How long did that take—for help to come?"

"For a while no one knew what had become of us. We waited for days, not knowing who would find us first, our boys or the enemy. Fortunately, the plane was well-equipped with medical supplies and food. When the Allied troops found us three days later, we'd managed to keep all of our patients alive and well."

"Thanks to hundreds of women like Aunt Sarah, more than a million soldiers were flown to safety to recover in hospitals," Frank said. "Because of their great skills and fearless commitment to helping others, Aunt Sarah and her fellow flight nurses saved all but a handful of those soldiers. So yeah, I'd have to say that qualifies as being a real hero—even beyond being my hero."

"I can't imagine doing what you did," MaryAnn confessed. "I would have been too afraid to help anyone."

Aunt Sarah studied MaryAnn's face for a moment and then replied: "You know, it's a funny thing about frightening situations.

When you're right there, you're so scared you can't even feel it, so you just do what you have to do. I was never calmer in my life than when that plane went down. I really can't explain why. Somehow, though, I knew God was with us, taking care of us, and would give me the strength I needed to do what I had to do."

"Look, here's a picture!" MaryAnn exclaimed excitedly. "This is you, isn't it, Aunt Sarah? You're wearing this very uniform."

Sarah examined the photograph and smiled. "Yes, that's me."

"Look how young you are," MaryAnn gushed. "And beautiful. Look at you with this handsome young officer."

Frank leaned in with great interest. "And who's this handsome young man with his arms wrapped around you? He seems quite smitten with you. That isn't Uncle Matthew, is it?"

Sarah chuckled. "No, that's not Matthew," she admitted. "It's his best friend, Trevor Parks."

Frank's eyebrow shot upward. "Sounds like a story to me. What happened to him? How'd you end up with Uncle Matt instead?"

"The three of us were assigned passage back to the U.S. on a hospital ship. We were all so excited to be going home—and together. But then at the last moment, Matt and I were reassigned. It was two more weeks before we were finally able to get out on a plane. When we got back to California, we learned that Trevor hadn't made it home."

Her eyes glistened with the memory. She looked at the picture for a long time, gently touching Trevor's face with her gnarled finger. "It wasn't supposed to happen like that," she said in a low voice. "The Red Cross flag was clearly flying. The enemy wasn't supposed to attack, but they did. A Japanese plane strafed the ship, and Trevor was struck by a bullet and killed."

Frank leaned down and gave his aunt a long hug. "I'm sorry, Aunt Sarah."

"So was I," Sarah responded. "It wasn't what I had planned for Trevor—or for my life. But God knew what He was doing. I found out I'm stronger than I thought I was . . . more resilient. I made a wonderful life with Matthew after that. I'm not sad about how my life turned out."

It was then that Sarah realized something important about her life. She would not let an unexpected change in plans defeat her. A broken hip wouldn't break her. She wasn't giving up her life, but embarking on a new adventure. She had stared down fear, hardship, and danger before without bowing in defeat: surely she could face the challenges of the Rainbow Senior Center with the same courage and dignity.

Frank kissed her forehead. "You're the bravest person I've ever met. You truly are my hero."

Sarah didn't feel like a hero. She didn't even feel that brave. But she did feel a renewed sense of determination and hope. She smiled contentedly. For her, it was enough.

Chapter Five

Aunts Can
Be Adopted

Never forget that you're wanted and chosen by
Me. You've been adopted into royalty and holiness.
I've called you out of darkness into purpose. You're
My heir. As My daughter, you share My treasures,
suffering, and glory. When you fear Me, I help
you to make the best choices for your life. May you
choose the way of truth and set your heart on My
laws. I'll set your heart free. By following Me and
My ways, you'll discover delight.

With My forever love,

Your Heavenly Father

—from 1 Peter 2:9; Romans 8:17; Psalm 119:30–35

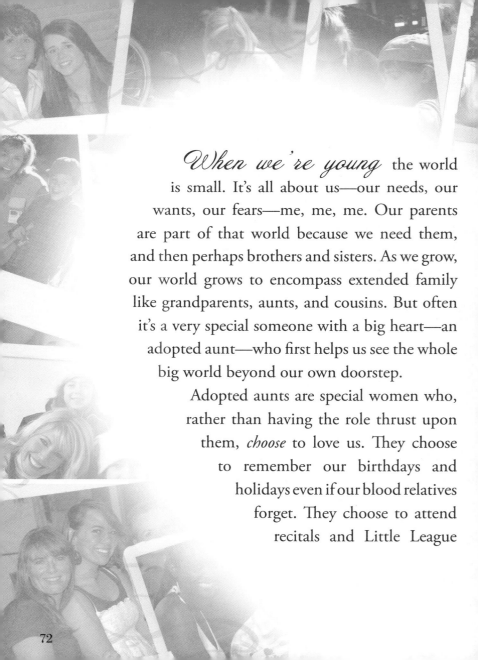

When we're young the world is small. It's all about us—our needs, our wants, our fears—me, me, me. Our parents are part of that world because we need them, and then perhaps brothers and sisters. As we grow, our world grows to encompass extended family like grandparents, aunts, and cousins. But often it's a very special someone with a big heart—an adopted aunt—who first helps us see the whole big world beyond our own doorstep.

Adopted aunts are special women who, rather than having the role thrust upon them, *choose* to love us. They choose to remember our birthdays and holidays even if our blood relatives forget. They choose to attend recitals and Little League games and cheer us on as if we were the greatest. They willingly open their hearts and their homes to us as we go through the awkward stages and trying times of life. They're always there to remind us that although the world is big, unknown, and at times scary, there will be lots of good new things out there too.

An unexpected change might be an unexpected opportunity. Something beyond our own control might be God's good plan for our lives. A leap of faith might find us landing on solid, pleasant ground. And a perfect stranger just might be a perfectly wonderful person—an adopted aunt—who will enrich our lives and open our eyes to a world of possibilities.

Yes, love is the magic key of life—not to get what we want but to become what we ought to be.

—Eileen Guder

What Was I Thinking?

It was another terrible, horrible day. Ten-year-old Camille was so deep in her misery when she stepped out through the big main doors at Polser Elementary that she didn't even notice the beauty of the warm spring day, only that the sun was in her eyes. Not wanting to hurry home or be forced to make pleasant small talk while walking with her friends, she had hung back—dawdling, as her mother would put it—until most of the other kids had left. She relished being left alone so she could wallow in the misery her stupid parents were causing her. She wondered how long it would take for them to realize how much their decision to move was hurting her—destroying her life—and change their minds. Perhaps if she—

"Camille," a voice interrupted her thoughts. "Camille!" The

call was more insistent. "You walked right past me. What are you thinking?" Surprised, Camille turned to see a woman balanced on a bike, pushing backward to catch up with her. The woman wore a bike helmet, goggles, and a scarf that worked together to obscure her face, but the curly black hair cascading down her back was unmistakable.

"Aunt Jane, is that you?" Camille asked tentatively.

"Yes, it's me. I've come to pick you up."

"Oh, my!" Camille exclaimed, her hand flying to her mouth in surprise when she got her first good look at the unusual bike as it pulled alongside her. "What *is* this?"

"It's a tandem," Aunt Jane announced joyfully, pulling the goggles from her face and allowing them to hang around her neck. "A bicycle built for two. Get on. I brought a helmet and goggles for you too."

It was *so* Aunt Jane, Camille thought as she put on the protective gear and climbed onto the seat with growing excitement. Aunt Jane had been her mom's best friend since before they were Camille's age, so she wasn't really an aunt in the usual family sense . . . but that seemed appropriate, since Jane was anything but usual! Camille's mother called her quirky; Camille's father called her weird. Camille just called her Aunt Jane, and she was probably her favorite of all her many more typical aunts.

It was strange at first, riding behind Aunt Jane. Camille could pedal or not: the bike didn't slow much or stop if she decided to rest her legs. Aunt Jane blocked her view of the path forward, although Camille was grateful to have the sun blocked from her eyes. But the most difficult thing to get used to was that, although her pair of handlebars gave her something to hold on to, they were absolutely useless for steering. That responsibility lay totally with Aunt Jane. Still, it took only a few minutes for Camille to relax and learn to enjoy the situation and the interesting scenery flying past.

She had no idea where they were going. They raced past the park, the duck pond, a new housing development, and a little creek with wildflowers dotting its banks. Before long Camille recognized Aunt Jane's neighborhood, and all too soon the ride was over.

Camille squealed with delight as they coasted to a stop in Aunt Jane's driveway. "I thought you'd enjoy taking the scenic route." Aunt Jane smiled, holding the bike steady so Camille could dismount.

"It was great!" Camille agreed wholeheartedly. "But what's going on?"

"Your mom said I could have you for the evening," Aunt Jane explained, using a key to open the front door. "If that's okay with you." She glanced back at Camille, who vigorously nodded her approval. "I figured you could help me make dinner, and then we'd just hang out—do whatever."

Camille tossed her goggles and helmet on the floor beside Aunt Jane's and followed her to the kitchen.

"I know it's kind of early, but bike riding makes me hungry," Aunt Jane said as she motioned for Camille to join her in washing her hands at the kitchen sink. "How do nachos sound?"

"I love nachos," Camille said enthusiastically.

"Great—you shred some cheese while I brown and season some chicken."

The smell of spicy seasonings made Camille's mouth water. She snitched a pinch of shredded cheese while Aunt Jane cut up tomatoes and peppers.

"Your mom said you're not very happy about the prospect of moving."

Camille wrinkled her nose and shoveled a larger sample of cheese into her mouth. "I *hate* the thought of moving. I'm not going to move—not if there's anything I can do to stop it."

"But Camille, you're moving less than a mile from your old house to a bigger, nicer house with a better backyard. What's not to like?"

"Everything!" Camille announced emphatically.

"Name one thing specifically."

"School. I'll have to change schools."

"You're finishing up fifth grade," Aunt Jane countered thoughtfully.

"You'd be going to a new school next year anyway."

"But at least it would be in the same district. All my friends would be going to the new school with me. Now I'll have to go to Blalack." She made a face.

"Hey, I went to Blalack!" Aunt Jane acted offended. "It's not such a bad school."

"That explains a lot," Camille said solemnly before breaking into laughter at the face Aunt Jane made.

"Your brother seems ready to move."

"All he cares about is football," Camille said, her mouth full of cheese. "He thinks he stands a better chance of playing varsity at Creek View High than at Hebron."

Aunt Jane handed Camille the block of cheese and motioned for her to shred some more to replace what she'd eaten. "We won't have enough for the nachos," she said good-naturedly. "What were you thinking?" Then she grew serious. "Things change, Camille, whether we want them to or not."

"But I like my friends," Camille said earnestly. "I don't want to lose them."

"Middle school is different from elementary," Aunt Jane explained. "You might not even see the friends you have now anyway. Friends grow and change and move on."

"Not mine," Camille said assuredly. "We're going to be friends forever—like you and Mom."

Aunt Jane smiled. "You won't be far from your friends," she consoled. "You'll still be able to see them—you'll be able to bike back to your old neighborhood. And your new bedroom is really nice. You'll even have your own bathroom. Trust me, in a few years that'll matter."

"It doesn't matter at all to me!" Camille said loudly. "I like my old bedroom just the way it is. I like the bathroom I have now. I like my backyard. I like everything just the way it is. I don't want anything to change!"

Aunt Jane spoke soothingly. "Change is hard for you. I remember you cried when your parents traded in your old Chevy."

"That was a good car," Camille said defensively; then, after seeing the amused look on Aunt Jane's face, added sheepishly, "I was five."

"And now you're ten," Aunt Jane said matter-of-factly. "Almost eleven. That's five more years to have learned that change can be wonderful and exciting. It's not something to fear but to embrace. You have a chance to expand your horizons, meet new people who could be your best friends for life. You can grow and learn and discover so much more to love!" Her eyes shone passionately, but Camille wasn't convinced.

"That house will never be my real home," she announced stubbornly.

"Like I'm not your 'real' aunt?"

The question stung Camille. She couldn't have loved Aunt Jane anymore if she were related by blood. This seemed personal to Aunt Jane. Could it be that by rejecting this new home, she was possibly rejecting another "Aunt Jane" in her life—something she could love and cherish that she just hadn't embraced yet?

Aunt Jane handed Camille a tub of sour cream. "Stir that up for me, will you?"

"Ew," Camille exclaimed when she removed the lid. "I think it's gone bad. It's green!"

Aunt Jane smiled. "Smell it," she commanded, sticking the container under Camille's nose. To Camille's surprise, it smelled like normal sour cream.

"But it looks—"

"Looks can be deceiving," Aunt Jane said mysteriously, her eyes dancing. She stuck her finger into the green sour cream and tasted it cautiously before licking her finger clean. "Tastes good to me," she declared. She produced a large bag of tortilla chips from her pantry.

"Hey," Camille blurted in surprise. "Those aren't the regular chips!"

Aunt Jane looked at them as if noticing for the first time that the chips were red and blue. "You're right," she admitted. "What was I thinking?"

"I don't think I like chips like that," Camille said unhappily.

"You won't know until you try them. Here, have one." She thrust a blue chip toward Camille's mouth. Camille hesitantly took a small bite and considered it carefully before changing her skeptical expression.

"Hey, this is good. It tastes just like a regular chip. It's a little saltier, though." She smiled. "I like that!"

By the end of their dinner, Camille had gamely tried lots of new or unusually presented foods and discovered that they weren't all that different from what she'd had before. She'd even tried a little onion and hot pepper on her nachos, and—although she'd never admit it to Aunt Jane—discovered that she actually kind of liked them. Maybe she was growing up a little, she mused. She also drank red-colored cream soda instead of the familiar white and ate purple lettuce and green taco sauce instead of red. But the real topper was when she helped Aunt Jane make fried ice cream for dessert. Fried ice cream! Camille had been convinced it was impossible to deep-fry ice cream without melting it, but she'd been proven wrong. Not only was it possible, but she decided it was the most delicious dessert she'd ever eaten.

She waved off Aunt Jane's offer of seconds. "I'm super full," she protested. "But it was super good." She paused and smirked at the look of satisfaction on Aunt Jane's face. "And Aunt Jane," she added softly, "I get what you're doing."

"What's that?" Aunt Jane asked playfully.

"I know you're showing me that I ought to give new things a chance—the new house and school."

"Do you think you could do that?" Aunt Jane was suddenly serious. "See this change as an opportunity for an exciting new adventure? It just might be fun."

Camille considered it for a moment, then smiled and nodded. "It just might be," she admitted. "I guess I haven't really given it a chance, have I?" She leaned in to Aunt Jane's warm embrace, and with a mischievous grin added, "What was I thinking?"

Chapter Six

Aunts Love
Uniquely

You are forever loved by Me. My love for you can never be cut off. And I empower you to give love. As you love others, you show that I am living in you, and My love is made perfect in you.

Loving you always and forever,
Your God of Love
—from Psalm 103:17; Romans 8:38–39; 1 John 4:11–12

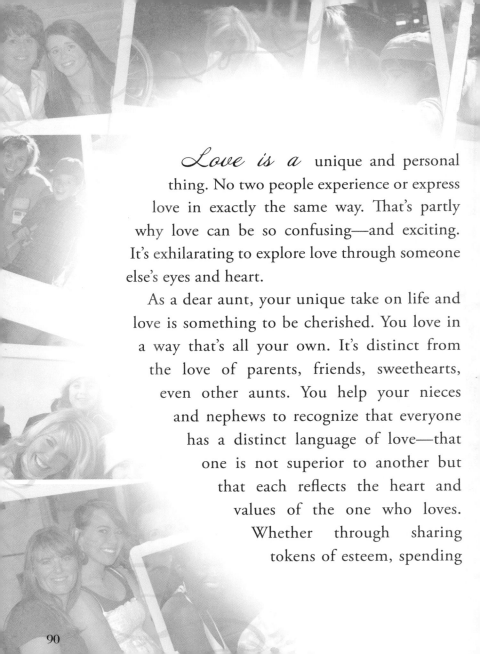

Love is a unique and personal thing. No two people experience or express love in exactly the same way. That's partly why love can be so confusing—and exciting. It's exhilarating to explore love through someone else's eyes and heart.

As a dear aunt, your unique take on life and love is something to be cherished. You love in a way that's all your own. It's distinct from the love of parents, friends, sweethearts, even other aunts. You help your nieces and nephews to recognize that everyone has a distinct language of love—that one is not superior to another but that each reflects the heart and values of the one who loves. Whether through sharing tokens of esteem, spending

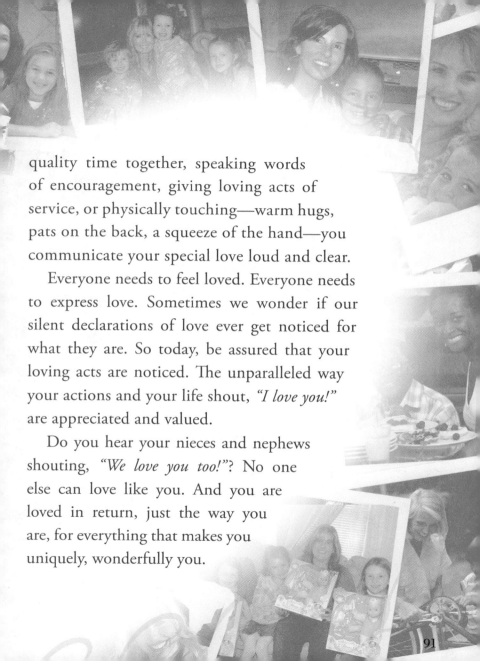

quality time together, speaking words of encouragement, giving loving acts of service, or physically touching—warm hugs, pats on the back, a squeeze of the hand—you communicate your special love loud and clear.

Everyone needs to feel loved. Everyone needs to express love. Sometimes we wonder if our silent declarations of love ever get noticed for what they are. So today, be assured that your loving acts are noticed. The unparalleled way your actions and your life shout, *"I love you!"* are appreciated and valued.

Do you hear your nieces and nephews shouting, *"We love you too!"*? No one else can love like you. And you are loved in return, just the way you are, for everything that makes you uniquely, wonderfully you.

Love's finest speech is
without words.

—HADEWIJCH OF
BRABANT

A Tale of Two Aunts

She'd told Aunt Peggy she was going to take a nap, but the truth was that Chelsea was hiding out: hiding from Uncle David's lighthearted joking when her heart was heavy. Hiding from the charade that everything was as it should be. Trying feverishly to figure out what had happened to make Aunt Paulette stop loving her.

Had she forgotten to send Aunt Paulette a thank-you note for her birthday gift? She didn't think so. Chelsea flopped onto the extra-high four-poster bed and stared forlornly at the ceiling. She fixated on a small crack in the old plaster directly above her. Was it new, or had she just not noticed it before, during the many summers since her mom had died that she'd spent time with Aunt Peggy? A dark thought crept into Chelsea's mind. Maybe the rift between herself and Aunt Paulette wasn't new. Maybe she just had been too young and naive to see it.

She rolled onto her side and tried to think back on past interactions with her aunt. It occurred to her that Aunt Paulette had not wanted to be hugged last Christmas. Aunt Paulette was never as huggable as Aunt Peggy, but Chelsea had thought it odd even then that she wouldn't even give her a little squeeze of affection.

Her eyes focused on the old photos standing watch over the bed from their perch atop the highboy dresser. The largest, her favorite, was of her mother as a young woman with her two sisters: Peggy, the older, and Paulette, the baby. Their smiles marked them as sisters. Apart from that, the three were so different that most people wouldn't have guessed they were related. Paulette had red hair and was thin as a candy cane, while Peggy was brunette and, well, not nearly as thin. As usual, Chelsea's mother, Pat, was somewhere in the middle.

Chelsea didn't remember a lot about her mother, but she loved to hear the stories from her two favorite aunts of what her mom was like. She liked it when Aunt Peggy told her she was like her mother, with her quick sense of humor, her dramatic flair, and her desire to help people. Her mother had been a nurse, and Chelsea was interested in pursuing a similar path—which is why, heading into her senior year of high school, Chelsea had been exploring options for college. She had narrowed it down to one in Ohio, just ninety miles from Aunt Peggy's, and another in New York City, where she could live with Aunt Paulette, if it worked out. She had hoped to make up her mind by visiting both schools this summer when she spent a week with each aunt—just like every summer. But rather than sounding excited about the possibility, Aunt Paulette's e-mails had urged her to seriously consider Ohio University—not NYU. And now this: Aunt Paulette had backed out of Chelsea's visit—actually uninvited her—and she didn't even have a good excuse. That is, unless you considered not loving your only niece anymore a good excuse, Chelsea thought, sulking.

She felt a growing sense of anger at herself for not having seen it sooner: how could she ever have thought that Aunt Paulette really loved her? Increasingly agitated, Chelsea felt compelled to check out another hunch. She knew Aunt Peg kept the old photo albums on the top shelf of the closet. She grabbed the wooden spindle desk chair and maneuvered it into the closet, then climbed on it and grabbed a stack of albums.

Back on the bed she tossed aside several albums that focused on Aunt Peggy's three boys and picked up a more feminine-looking album that appeared to be primarily about Chelsea. Quite a few pictures featured Chelsea with her mom, some with her mom and dad, and as she grew older, just with her dad. She saw a bunch of her with her cousins—honestly, was there a single picture of David Junior in existence where he wasn't making some goofy face?—and multiple shots of her with Aunt Peg: sitting on her lap, feeding the ducks, climbing the apple tree, making cookies together, playing games, blowing out birthday candles, and going to church all dressed up. But where were the pictures of her with Aunt Paulette? How had she failed to notice how absent Paulette seemed to be from her life? Chelsea was dumbfounded . . . and miserable.

She barely noticed the gentle knocking on the bedroom door and her aunt's muffled voice: "Chelsea, we heard a lot of creaking and banging up here. Is everything okay?"

"Aunt Peggy, come here and look at this." Chelsea's voice had a tone of righteous indignation.

"Oh, you've found your scrapbook," Aunt Peggy said, moving the other albums so she could sit beside Chelsea on the bed. "Isn't it done beautifully? So appropriate for a beautiful, favorite niece."

"Aunt Peggy, why doesn't Aunt Paulette like me anymore?" Chelsea asked bluntly. Her aunt looked stricken and remained silent, so Chelsea continued, "Did she ever . . . you know . . . really love me?"

"Chelsea! That's a terrible thing to say about your Aunt Paulette.

Of course she loves you. You know that. How can you even question her love?"

"Then why isn't she in any of these pictures?" Chelsea demanded, flipping through the scrapbook fiercely. "How many important events in my life was I too young or too preoccupied to notice that she skipped?"

"Honey," Peggy said, rescuing the book from Chelsea's rough handling. "Aunt Paulette made this book. She was at every event commemorated in here. She's the one who took the pictures, that's why she's not in them. Do you know how much time and effort it takes to put together a scrapbook like this? It's a beautiful gift of love!"

The realization hit Chelsea hard. Well, of course. Aunt Paulette was the artistic one, the photographer. Why hadn't she thought of that? Still, there were so many other signs . . .

"But she doesn't love me like you do, Aunt Peggy," Chelsea protested. "You're not afraid to get dirty or mess up your hair. You hug me and go for hikes and climb trees with me. Can you imagine Aunt Paulette doing any of those things?"

"No," Peggy agreed. "Paulette doesn't love you like I do: she loves you like Paulette does."

Chelsea looked at Aunt Peggy quizzically.

"There are lots of different ways to show love, Chelsea," Aunt Peggy said softly. "Paulette loves art and culture. She shares those things with you. Didn't she take you to *Mama Mia* on Broadway last summer?" Chelsea looked down and nodded. "Hasn't she taken you to lots of shows and museums and art galleries and festivals?"

"Yes, but those are things Aunt Paulette likes to do. Wouldn't she be doing those things anyway, whether I went with her or not?"

Aunt Peggy's eyes flashed with anger. "Do you know how much it costs to see a Broadway show?" Chelsea shook her head. "A *lot*! She probably spent more than three hundred dollars to take you to dinner and a show."

Chelsea was truly shocked, but she couldn't let it go. "Yeah, but—"

"But nothing!" Aunt Peggy shut her down. "It's not cheap living in New York. You have no idea how much of a sacrifice it is for your aunt to share something she loves with someone she loves . . . you heard me, *loves*!

"C'mon," Aunt Peggy said more softly, leaning close to Chelsea. "What's really up with you? Never before have you doubted that your aunts love you."

Chelsea stuck out her bottom lip in a pout and pondered how to make her aunt understand. "Something's just not right," she said finally.

Aunt Peggy took a deep breath and let it out slowly, noisily. "Okay, what makes you say that?"

Tears filled Chelsea's eyes, and she leaned her head on Aunt Peg's ample shoulder. "Oh, Aunt Peg, why didn't she want me to come visit this year? Why doesn't she call like she used to? Why does she just send e-mails? She doesn't want me to go to school in New York—I wouldn't have to live with her if she doesn't want me. She doesn't even seem to want me close. She wouldn't even hug me at Christmas." All the accusations came tumbling out in one painful torrent.

Aunt Peggy gathered Chelsea into her arms and held her tight, rocking gently, rubbing her back comfortingly.

"Child, child, child," Peggy soothed gently. "Something's not right, but it's not what you think. Aunt Paulette didn't want to tell you, but I think it's best you know."

Chelsea pulled away from her aunt so she could look into her eyes. It unnerved her to see they had filled with tears.

"Paulette is sick," Peggy said quietly.

"What's wrong?" Chelsea pressed, fearful of the answer.

"She had surgery just after Thanksgiving last year. She was still sore and healing at Christmas. That's why she couldn't let you hug her."

"What's the matter?"

"She's on a second round of treatments this summer," Peggy continued. "It takes a lot out of her. There's nothing she likes better than to have you with her, but this summer she needs to focus on getting well."

"Is it . . . is it . . . like Mom?" Chelsea stammered.

"Yes, it's breast cancer, but the prognosis is hopeful. Paulette didn't want you to have to carry that load again." Aunt Peggy wiped tears from her eyes.

"So she wanted me to go to school near you—"

"Just in case. She wanted us to be together. Didn't want to be a burden on you." Both Chelsea and Peggy were crying openly now. Chelsea burned with shame for having doubted Aunt Paulette's love.

"We have to go to her," Chelsea pleaded. "We have to be with her . . . show her we love her."

"There are lots of ways to show love," Aunt Peggy responded. "We should respect Paulette's wishes and let her do this her way. Let's think of a different way to show her that we love her."

It was the end of summer. Beneath her scarf, Paulette's hair was starting to grow back and, like Samson, her strength was returning with it. At the sound of the doorbell, her Siamese cat jumped from her chest to the floor. She peered through the peephole to see a deliveryman holding a package. With a little concern, but also great interest, she opened the door to sign for the package. It was from Chelsea.

Ripping the paper off, she was delighted to see that it was an album, a scrapbook, with lots of photos: Chelsea and Peggy by the old apple tree, by the pond, in front of the farmhouse. There was David manning the grill. Paulette felt a twinge of sadness that she hadn't been a part of things. She turned the page and gasped. It was her in this picture . . . and that one too, and these..

Dumbfounded, she paged through the book. Some of the photos had been altered artfully: it almost looked like she was really on the farm. Others were purposefully comical: her head superimposed on Peggy's thicker body. She laughed out loud. Then, quickly, the laughter turned to tears as she understood what she was seeing. Here she was at the opera with Chelsea; there they seemed to be at Shakespeare in the Park. Her time "with Chelsea" that summer seemed to include dressing up and going shopping, fine dining, visiting an art museum, and taking a pottery class. In most cases it appeared that Peggy had been her stand-in; but in some photos

Paulette had been Photoshopped in alongside them both. Peggy and Chelsea had spent their time together doing things that Paulette would love and then, in their love, had included her in each outing. Chelsea wasn't with her in New York, but she was with her in spirit. What could be better? The things she loved best with the people she loved most.

Paulette got the message loud and clear. She was loved, and she loved Chelsea even more for it.

Chapter Seven

Aunts Inspire

I've prepared you in advance for the special
objectives I created you to accomplish.
Challenge others to love and good deeds.
Your life adds flavor. You are a shining light.
Continue to be an example for others. Live
your life so others will see the good things you
do and praise Me.

Guiding you every day,
Your God of All Hope
—from Ephesians 2:10; Hebrews 10:24; Matthew 5:13–16

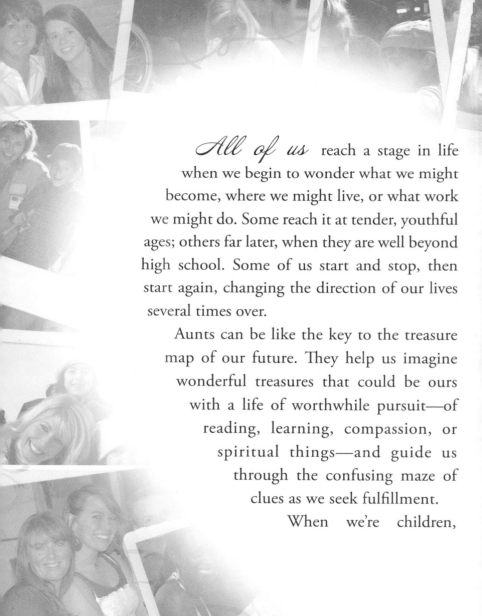

All of us reach a stage in life when we begin to wonder what we might become, where we might live, or what work we might do. Some reach it at tender, youthful ages; others far later, when they are well beyond high school. Some of us start and stop, then start again, changing the direction of our lives several times over.

Aunts can be like the key to the treasure map of our future. They help us imagine wonderful treasures that could be ours with a life of worthwhile pursuit—of reading, learning, compassion, or spiritual things—and guide us through the confusing maze of clues as we seek fulfillment.

When we're children,

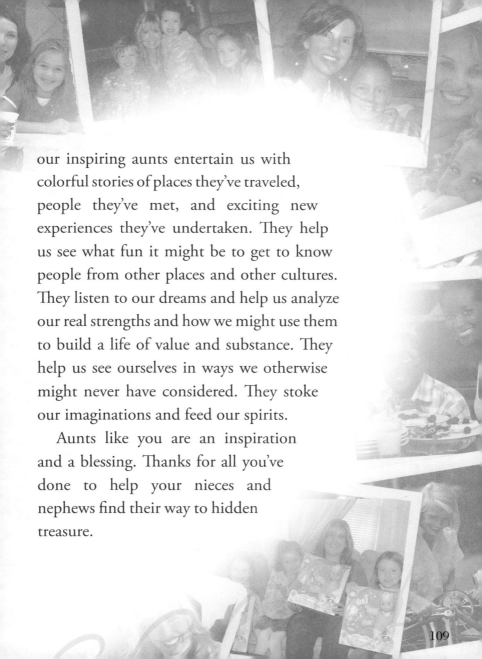

our inspiring aunts entertain us with colorful stories of places they've traveled, people they've met, and exciting new experiences they've undertaken. They help us see what fun it might be to get to know people from other places and other cultures. They listen to our dreams and help us analyze our real strengths and how we might use them to build a life of value and substance. They help us see ourselves in ways we otherwise might never have considered. They stoke our imaginations and feed our spirits.

Aunts like you are an inspiration and a blessing. Thanks for all you've done to help your nieces and nephews find their way to hidden treasure.

Encouragement is oxygen to
the soul.

—George M. Adams

Aunt Vera's Purse

As Mike settled into his room, he was happy to hear Benny Goodman's band playing some pretty lively swing music. He knew how much his Aunt Vera loved swing (she'd been quite a dancer in her day), and it made him smile. He had flown in from Italy and, after several delays at the airport, was glad to finally be here to help his aunt put her affairs in order. Aunt Vera had always been special to Mike, and he was more than happy to help her with her requests.

After unpacking his bags, he went downstairs to find his aunt sitting on the porch preparing an aromatic cup of tea.

"Don't you just love Benny Goodman?" She beamed when he sat down at the little table next to her. "Oh, how your Uncle Jack and I loved to dance. It was one of the best things we did together."

"I always liked watching you dance," Mike responded. "You two were so much fun. I miss Uncle Jack a lot."

"Yes, me too." Aunt Vera sighed. "But life goes on, and we still have great things to enjoy. Why, having you here with me is one of those." She smiled.

"Mike," she continued more thoughtfully, "you know you've always been special to me . . . "

Mike smiled warmly but dropped his eyes self-consciously. He felt the same way about Aunt Vera, and he hoped his smile communicated that.

"Is there anything particular you'd like from me after I'm gone . . . anything with special meaning you'd like to keep as a reminder of our times together?"

Instantly Mike knew what he wanted above anything else. "Aunt Vera, if you still have that carpetbag of a purse you carried when I was little, I'd really appreciate having that."

Aunt Vera laughed with great humor. "My old purse? You want my old purse? Yes, I still have it, but what would a handsome young man like yourself want with an old woman's purse—is there something you wanted to tell me?"

Mike couldn't help but laugh with her. "As a matter of fact, yes," he said. "I *do* have something to tell you. Remember the first time I stayed at your house. . . ?"

Seven-year-old Mikey's parents had gone out of town for the weekend and left him in the charge of his Great-Aunt Vera. It was all new to Mikey: he'd never been without his parents for such a long time, and Aunt Vera was . . . well . . . she was not like anyone else Mikey knew. He felt shy—and miserable.

But Aunt Vera seemed perfectly delighted to have him. "Mikey," she said with a smile, "what shall we do this weekend? We have so many happy hours to spend together, and we need to make a plan. Shall we bake cookies or hike in the woods? Uncle Jack won't be home for a while, so we'll have to make up our own fun."

Mikey could think of nothing but getting out of there, but Aunt Vera had plenty of ideas. She walked over to her gigantic purse—her signature accessory—and ushered him along with her. "Now, let's look in here and see what we can find," she said. "I'm sure there are some surprises hidden in here somewhere." She dug through her purse as young Mike stood and watched, not quite sure what to expect.

"Do you like to play pretend games?" she asked. "Let's pretend my purse is a treasure chest that we found hidden under the house. Who do you think could have left this treasure for us?"

Mikey thought this was silly, but he played along to make his aunt happy. "Maybe somebody who lived in this house a long time ago?" he offered.

"You're absolutely right!" Aunt Vera beamed. "This house once belonged to a sea captain. He probably met some pirates out on the high seas and buried this amazing treasure so no one would find it."

In spite of his best efforts to stay miserable, Mikey was starting to get excited at the thought of buried pirate treasure. "Maybe the pirates are still looking for the treasure!"

Aunt Vera leaned over and grabbed a blanket. She huddled up with Mikey, and they looked around to make sure no pirates were watching. "Let's see what's in here," she whispered conspiratorially.

The first thing she pulled out was a black eye patch. She handed it to Mikey. "You'd better put this on."

Wide-eyed, Mikey donned the patch and waited breathlessly to see what else they might find.

Aunt Vera put her hand back in the purse and pulled out a piece of paper that looked a hundred years old. Mikey gasped. "What's that?" he whispered.

Aunt Vera blew on it as if to clear the dust of the ages and carefully unfolded the paper. Now Aunt Vera's eyes were wide as saucers. "Mikey, it's a treasure map—and it's for this house!"

"What?" Mikey whispered in amazement. "What does it say? What do we do?"

Aunt Vera cleared her throat but still spoke softly. "We have to go to the grandfather clock and open the locked chamber. Another clue is hidden there."

Mikey looked at the grandfather clock. "Where's the key?"

"It's somewhere on the clock. Go see if you can find it."

Mikey walked up to the clock that stood more than six feet tall. He couldn't see a key. Then he realized that the key they needed was not like the one that would get him into his house with his parents; they needed a special key. "Oh, there it is, I think. It looks almost like one of the numbers on the clock. It's curled up like a number six with a key on the tip of it," Mikey exclaimed, his voice getting louder. "Can you reach it, Aunt Vera? Is that the key?"

Aunt Vera was a petite woman, so even she had to stretch a bit to get the key. She put it in Mikey's hand. "That's it," she said. "Let's open the clock."

Mikey had to work to get the key in just right, but he finally heard the old clock chamber open.

"You look first," his aunt said.

Mikey opened the narrow door and peeked in. He couldn't see anything that looked like a treasure. Finally he ran his hand across a nearly hidden space behind one of the inner workings of the clock . . . and discovered a tiny box. "It's a box," he whispered. "It probably has the next clue in it." By this time Mikey had forgotten they were playing pretend games. He was starting to truly believe there was a treasure in his aunt's house.

They carried the box over to the one lamp faintly sending its glow throughout the room. Taking a deep breath, Mikey carefully lifted the tiny latch on the box. Inside was something silver. "What's this?" he asked. "It looks like a knob off of something."

Aunt Vera looked thoughtful. "I don't rightly know," she said. "Let's go look in the kitchen and see if there's anything this knob might belong to."

Mikey was in the kitchen searching high and low before Aunt Vera could even get to the hallway. "It's not from any of the cupboards or the doors," he exclaimed, entranced with the mystery.

Aunt Vera looked around the room and then tapped Mikey on the shoulder. "I think I've spotted it." Mikey's eyes followed her gaze to an old lamp that had two pull chains—but only one had a knob on the end. A knob just like the one Mikey held in his hand.

They both walked over to the lamp, and Mikey replaced the knob. "I don't see a clue, though," he said, peeking over and into the lamp.

"Let's turn the light on," his aunt suggested. "We'll be able to see better then."

When the lamp came on, they stood back and looked. There on the lampshade was another clue! A note was pinned to the underside of the shade: "The treasure you seek is in the antique, and if you would find it, you must go behind it."

"What's an antique?" Mikey nearly shouted. "How can we find the antique?"

Aunt Vera laughed. "Antiques are old things. The house is full of them, so that's a tough one." She looked around. "Well, it can't be any of the really small ones, since we have to go behind it. What antiques can we get behind?"

Mikey scanned the room. Nothing seemed likely, so they left the kitchen and went back to the living room. A bunch of old chairs and tables filled the room, and there was the grandfather clock, but nothing they could really get behind. "Let's try your room," Mikey suggested and ran toward his aunt's bedroom.

They agreed that it couldn't be the bed, since they'd only be able to get beneath it, not behind it. The dresser was flush to the wall and too hard to move, so it probably wasn't the right antique either. At last Mikey spotted something. "The mirror!" he shouted. "I bet it's behind that big stand-up mirror."

Aunt Vera smiled as they worked their way behind the big old mirror. There, in plain sight, was another old-looking piece of paper. Aunt Vera read its message aloud: "A treasure brings pleasure with speed when you read."

Mikey looked at his aunt. "What does that mean?"

Aunt Vera put her hand on her forehead and seemed to be trying to think very hard. Then suddenly she grabbed Mikey's hand and walked him back around the mirror and toward the door. "I think I've got it! Do you remember seeing anything lying on your bed when we put away your suitcase earlier?"

Mikey didn't remember. "Let's go see," he said. Running to the